Letters in Wartime

Letters in Wartime

Kenneth Brown and Stephen Scriver

Playwrights Canada Press
Toronto • Canada

Playwrights Canada Press
The Canadian Drama Publisher
215 Spadina Avenue, Suite 230, Toronto, Ontario CANADA M5T 2C7
416-703-0013 fax 416-408-3402
orders@playwrightscanada.com • www.playwrightscanada.com

Financial support provided by the taxpayers of Canada and Ontario through the Canada Council for the Arts and the Department of Canadian Heritage through the Book Publishing Industry Development Programme, and the Ontario Arts Council.

Canada

The Canada Council for the Arts
Le Conseil des Arts du Canada

Ontario Arts Council
Conseil des Arts de l'Ontario

Production Editor/Cover design: JLArt

Library and Archives Canada Cataloguing in Publication

Brown, Kenneth, 1954-
Letters in wartime / Kenneth Brown, Stephen Scriver.

A play.
ISBN 0-88754-778-8

1. World War, 1939-1945--Aerial operations, Canadian--Drama.
I. Scriver, Stephen, 1947- II. Title.

PS8553.R68727L48 2005 C812'.54 C2005-904169-2

First edition: July 2005.
Printed and bound by AGMV Marquis at Quebec, Canada.

The technical advisor about wartime flying was Wally McSween, himself a former Lancaster pilot, to whose memory we dedicate this publication of Letters in Wartime.

Introduction to Letters in Wartime

Stephen Scriver

Kenneth Brown and Stephen Scriver were veterans of the hockey wars when they first met in 1990. Brown had written, produced and acted in his spectacularly successful one-man play, *Life After Hockey*, while Scriver's best-selling collections of hockey poems, *All Star Poet!* and *More All Star Poet*! were staples in Canadian schools and dressing rooms.

It was another connection, however, that brought them together creatively. They were the sons of veterans, and in their first conversations they discovered they both had been profoundly disturbed by the CBC production of the McEwen brothers' documentary, "The Valour and the Horror." As Brown put it: "The film angered not a few veterans of the war, who felt that their sacrifices and those of their comrades, were degraded by the film's apparent message: that the policy of bombing Germany, promoted by 'Butcher' Harris, had little strategic effect on the war's outcome." They felt a response was necessary.

At the 1993 Edmonton Fringe Festival, the idea was hatched that they would write and stage a play in response to "The Valour and the Horror" at the 1994 Fringe. *Letters in Wartime* was the result.

The writing process was collaborative at two stages. The play was first mapped out scene by scene. Brown, who had trained as a pilot, claimed the flying scenes, while Scriver, the researcher, provided much of the play's historical spine through incident and anecdote. Both men were ardent story collectors and tellers, and many of the names and events in the play were based on the recollections of veterans they had met. Foremost among these was their friend, the late actor Wally McSween, who flew Lancaster and Halifax bombers twenty-eight times over enemy territory in World War II. One of the great pleasures for the writers was having Wally attend several productions of the play.

After going their separate ways to write, Brown and Scriver came together again in the editing phase. Both men agree that the brutality and honesty necessary for the blue pencil process forged what has become an enduring friendship.

The obvious choices to play the roles of Allen and Moira for the first production were, of course, Kenneth and Michele Brown. Michele's pregnancy, however, necessitated the search for a new Moira, and Elizabeth McLaughlin came on board. During the first reading of the play, Elizabeth revealed that her uncle had not only been an RCAF Spitfire pilot during the war, but had been a prisoner of war at Stalag Luft 3, the POW camp from which The Great Escape was carried out.

The first production at the 1994 Edmonton Fringe Festival was staged, appropriately enough, in the Strathcona Legion Hall, and during eleven performances, including four in holdover, the audience response was tremendous. Colin McLean, the respected Edmonton drama critic, picked it as the finest production of that year's Fringe. It went on to win the drama community's Elizabeth Sterling Award for the best new Fringe work of 1994.

In the initial programme notes, Brown observed: "My personal reasons for wanting to do this play all have to do with honouring the superlative heroism of the Canadian men and women who traded their hard but simple provincial lives for years of privation and death. As they came of age, so did the nation.

"War is not good. I've never met a real warrior who thought it was. In the words of the late Roger Davies: 'Modern warfare is a prolonged industrial accident.' But I believe that wars bring out great qualities in people, and that there are some wars that have to be fought. The conflict against the Third Reich was one. Canadians accepted this terrible duty and fought."

Scriver added: "My hometown, Wolseley, SK, was less than 1000 souls, of whom over 100 served in WWII, and 21 sacrificed their young lives. Being surrounded by vets, including my dad, I learned to be a good listener, a collector of stories, and when I joined my own struggles on the hockey rink, a storyteller. I am thankful to have been given the chance to share some of the stories I collected. I have looked after these stories, and they will look after me."

As of the publication of this play, it has been staged six times: 1994 Edmonton Fringe (Ad Astra Productions and THEATrePUBLIC), Edmonton, 1995 (Workshop West), Morrisburg, ON, 1995 (Upper Canada Playhouse), Alberta Tour, 1997 (THEATrePUBLIC), Kelowna, BC, 2003 (Sunshine Theatre Productions), and Saskatoon, SK, 2005 (By The Book Productions).

Elizabeth McLaughlin, Kenneth Brown

photo by Thomas Turner, courtesy of THEATrePUBLIC

Production Information

Letters in Wartime had its first mainstage production by Upper Canada Playhouse, Morrisburg, Ontario, in September 1995 with the following company:

ALLAN Shaun Clarke MOIRA Elizabeth Goodyear.
Directed by Donnie Bowes

It was also produced by Workshop West Theatre at the Kaasa Theatre in the Jubilee Auditorium, Edmonton, Alberta, in November 1995 with the following company:

ALLAN John Ullyatt MOIRA Tanis Dolman
Director: David Mann
Stage Manager: Cheryl Millikin
Sound Design: David Clarke
Lighting/Set Design: Melinda Sutton

The premiere production of *Letters in Wartime* was a co-production of Ad Astra Productions and THEATrePUBLIC at Strathcona Legion Hall, Edmonton Fringe Festival, Edmonton, Alberta, in August 1994 with the following company:

ALLAN Kenneth Brown MOIRA Elizabeth McLaughlin
Director: Jim DeFelice
Stage Manager: Rob Trousdell
Production by S. Scriver, R. Trousdell & Co.

A later production by THEATrePUBLIC toured within Alberta. It starred Kenneth Brown as ALLAN and Michele Brown as MOIRA.

Other productions include: Sunshine Theatre Company, Kelowna, BC, in October, 2003, starring Daniel Arnold and Medina Hahn, directed by David Mann; and By the Book Productions, Saskatoon, SK, in January 2005, starring Skye Brandon and Clare Middleton, directed by John D. Huston.

Characters

Allan Staunton
Moira Lyons

Letters In Wartime

Prelude

Glenn Miller's "Moonlight Serenade."

On stage, two acting areas:

Stage right, a 1940s period writing desk and chair, behind which is an armchair beside a side-table upon which is a radio. The radio is practical, and will play occasional news reports. There is also a coat rack.

Stage left, a military-style steel writing desk and chair. A little downstage and to the left of this is a trunk marked "Staunton, A.W." Out of this box come ALLAN's changes of clothes. ALLAN also has a coat rack.

At centre-stage is a third acting area, which represents the train station, and the street in front of the chapel.

As the lights come down, a collage of sound: Chamberlain announcing "Peace In Our Time," Hitler giving his "Germany for the Germans" speech, the announcement of the invasion of Poland, Britain joins the war, Canada's declaration, the song "The Siegfried Line," Vera Lynn singing "The White Cliffs of Dover," Churchill's "Some chicken! Some neck!" speech to parliament, sound bytes from Dunkirk, announcement of Pearl Harbour, Roosevelt's "Infamy" speech; Christmas 1941, message from Mackenzie King.

The collage resolves in the music, "We'll Meet Again," and the sound of a steam train arriving at the station. The sound of steam huffing under:

ACT I – First Movement: Beginnings

Departure.

ALLAN Well.

MOIRA You look swell. In uniform.

ALLAN No wings yet, though.

MOIRA No.

ALLAN It's too bad about the University. Maybe you'll get a chance to go back next year.

MOIRA Well, Mom and Dad need me right now.

Short pause.

ALLAN Peter will be all right. I'm sure you'll be hearing something.

MOIRA Yes…

ALLAN Missing in Action doesn't mean dead. Hong Kong must be complete chaos, and who knows how the Japanese are dealing with their prisoners. I mean, you know, administration, and so on. They can't even pronounce our names. He'll make it just so I can rib him about dating his sister.

MOIRA Will you see Norman, do you suppose?

ALLAN No, I don't think so. Hardly any chance of being put on the same base. I think the conductor's waving.

MOIRA I'm glad you asked me to come and see you off.

ALLAN Are you? You look pretty in that dress. More than pretty. How about a kiss?

MOIRA Not in front of everyone.

They kiss. Pause.

ALLAN I meant to tell you. About that Saturday. What I said, in the car…

MOIRA I don't want to think about.... What I would feel if.... Just promise me...?

ALLAN What?

MOIRA Don't promise me anything.

ALLAN Promise me.

MOIRA What? *(beat)* What??

ALLAN Promise me you'll write. And take good care of yourself.

MOIRA Yes, I will. I will. For you.

The sound of a steam whistle. They kiss. Black.

Light. Two chairs. He sits writing. She recites a letter she has composed:

MOIRA *(writing)* Dear Allan. Wouldn't you know it? I'm hardly home from the train station and I can already feel how much I'm going to miss you. I have so much I want to tell you.

Pause. She can't think of anything to write.

When we kissed.... In front of all those people in the station. I felt like we... had wings.

Pause. She speaks to herself:

I felt like Andromache: "She stood beside close to him, letting her tears fall, and clung to his hand, and called him by name...." Why did I have to wait till he was leaving to feel that?

She writes:

Dr. Wilmot was wonderfully kind when I told him I wouldn't be at his lectures anymore. He said he had been grateful to have one enthusiastic Classics student. He gave me a copy of Homer's *Iliad*. "This book may be old, but it's not out of date," he said.

We have heard...

ALLAN & MOIRA *(together, he reading, she writing)* ...from Norman's family that he has been posted to a Spitfire squadron, isn't that dashing? And no, you have no need to be jealous. Must close now. Mother is just coming in from her church meeting…

ALLAN *(reading)* Best love…

MOIRA *(writing)* Best…. Love,

ALLAN & MOIRA *(together)* Moira.

ALLAN "Best love." Best. Love.

He hesitantly smells the envelope. It smells good.

Does that mean she *sends* me best love, or that I *am* her best love? And what does she mean, I have no need to be jealous? SPITfires! God.

He takes pen in hand, prepares to write.

(to himself) Is this supposed to be a… love letter…?

Pause.

I don't know how to write a love letter.

(writes) "Dear Moira: It was good kissing you…" Jesuus. *(Pause. He tries again.)* "Southern Alberta is very flat around here." Jesus!

He takes a breath, tries again.

Well, here we are, pounding the pencils and trying to be good students. Since we arrived, they've done everything they can to convince us of two things: first, that we are no longer civilians, and second, that whatever it is we are, we're no damn good at it. We certainly don't seem to be pilots—I don't think that anyone plans to trust us with an airplane during our military careers. Instead, they're teaching us the theory, 'though what value that's going to be in a dogfight against the Germans isn't exactly clear. Maybe we're supposed to bore them to death.

At night, when the lights go out, some smart-ass will yell out, "anybody from the West here." Some enthusiastic Westerner will yell out, "I'm from the West," and then all the Easterners will yell, well I won't say what they yell, but what they mean is "fornicate the West!" Whatever they call this training, it isn't for polite society.

Anyhow, the food is good. And there's lots of it, which is a pleasant change. In fact, I'm going to close this letter now because we have a mess call coming up.

Pause.

Look, I know that Norman and you had this understanding…

(to himself) Understanding…

He erases. He writes.

Glad to hear that Norman is doing so well. *(He is anything but glad.)* And hello to whoever… *(erases)* "Whomever. Best Wishes,

ALLAN & MOIRA *(together)* Allan.

MOIRA *(to herself)* Norman. Who I haven't heard from since September. "Best Wishes"?

She writes:

Dear Allan… *(erases)* My Dear Allan… *(erases)* My Dear Friend… *(erases)* My Dear Friend Allan… *(erases)*

Dear Allan,

It was good to get a letter from you so soon. I'm sure it's hard to get time to write. I'll bet you're all very dashing as you march around, keeping up the local girls' morale.

(to herself) I hope that's the only thing you're keeping up. *(laughs, then:)* Oh my.

(writing) How well I know what you mean about plentiful food. All my life it seems I've been scrimping and getting along with nearly nothing. I don't know what we'd have done during the thirties if Dad didn't hunt and Mom hadn't been a crackerjack gardener. Starved, I suppose. Still, I never want to taste moose meat again for the rest of my life.

The Japanese have taken Bahrain. Their progress through Malaysia has been startling. Thank God the Germans have decided to take on Joe Stalin, I hope they're as frozen as we are here.

ALLAN *(writing)* Elementary Flying Training School,

High River, Alberta

Dear Moira,

I don't think I chose the right service. Maybe I should re-muster for the Army. Had my first training flight in a Tiger Moth this morning, with a hard-bitten old (well, thirtyish) pilot who would prefer to be flying a Hurricane against the Germans. We took her up to seven thousand, and then he says, "down we go," and pulled over into a spin. It was like the movies, the world spinning in front of the windscreen. I had vertigo like crazy.

I feel like an idiot at the controls, nothing makes sense. They tell me this should change. If it doesn't, I'll be washed out and end up a tail-gunner in some hulking great bomber.

The prairies are so beautiful from the air. You can see all the mountain ranges from seven thousand feet, the world looks so perfect, you can't believe this training is for killing people.

MOIRA *(writing)* January 31st, 1942

Dear Allan,

The Russians are holding their own against the Germans on the Don River. If the weather is anything like it is in Alberta, I'll bet they're regretting that Hitler ever got the second front idea. And speaking of second fronts, I've been thinking about going out to work. Dot wants to get an apartment somewhere in Edmonton, near the base. I haven't told Dad yet about either plan. He's very old-fashioned about women working. You're not, are you? And once he hears about me moving out, he'll hit the roof. So I'm taking it one step at a time.

By the way, how DO you feel about women working?

ALLAN *(writing)* Dear Moira,

In response to your previous question: just fine. In fact, I'm all for a fellow being supported and lazing about while the women do the work.

Soloed on Saturday. I feel like a million bucks, I greased the landing with the whole gang watching. I'm starting to feel like this flying stuff could be fun. If all goes well, I'll be finished EFTS in a few weeks, and then I might get some leave. How about a date with a dashing Spitfire pilot? I've been doing a lot better on aerobatics. I think they might believe I'm fighter pilot material.

(to himself, delighted) I scared the crap out of myself this morning. Austin and I were bullshitting each other about flying under the bridge down near Nanton. They say the span is only fifty feet, and the deck is only twenty-five odd feet above the water. So Austin says, "Staunton, you wouldn't have the guts to fly under that span," and I told him to follow me if he had the guts. We chased each other once we got out of sight of the tower. The guys are always doing that, pulling fake dog-fights, practicing Immelman turns on each other. In a Tiger, you feel the wind in your face, it's like flying in the Great War, you pull that stick over and roll her, and you feel just like Billy Frigging Bishop.

We finished by finding our way to the Old Man River. We flew down low into the valley, following the contour of the river. I was pretending it was a train line somewhere, and I was machine-gunning a Kraut munitions train.

I was side-slipping around curves, turning the Moth on its side, pulling up to clear obstacles and letting the engine bite into the air. If I had made one mistake, I'd have been dead. I loved it.

MOIRA *(writing)* February 10th, 1942

Dearest Allan,

I don't know how to tell you this except to tell you—the Feniaks just got a telegram saying that Norman has been confirmed Killed in Action. It didn't give many details, something about him being shot down while strafing a train in France.

It seems like a nightmare. I've seen the notices for others in the *Journal*, but the names have never meant anything until now. A memorial service will be held on March 3rd. I hope you can get home. I don't want to go through this without you.

Please write soon. I think about you constantly,

Love,

Moira

ALLAN *(writing)* Dear Moira,

I can't tell you how sorry I am to hear of Norman's death. I will be home in three weeks for a few days before Service Flying School. Please keep me posted about the memorial. Let me know if there's anything I can do.

I have been posted to train on dual-engine aircraft, which probably means bombers.

MOIRA *(interrupts, speaking to herself)* Thank God, he's being posted to bomber training. Surely he'll be safer in bombers.

ALLAN *(to himself)* Because they're losing bomber crews at such an incredible rate.

(resuming his letter) I remember Norman with great admiration. He was a real leader and a man of deep conviction. It sounds corny, but I believe he gave his life in a struggle for democracy.

I am committed to taking up his battle if I can.

(to himself) And I will never fill his shoes.

Edmonton. ALLAN and MOIRA are outside the chapel after Norman Feniak's memorial service. MOIRA is preoccupied. She is thinking of Hector and Andromache. ALLAN is trying to work up his courage to propose.

MOIRA It was a nice lunch…

ALLAN Uh?

MOIRA Did you get a chance to speak to the Feniaks?

ALLAN Ya…. Mrs. Feniak couldn't even look at my face… just kept staring at my buttons…

MOIRA "Funerals are for the living. The dead care not that we mourn for them."

ALLAN I'll bet Norman was wearing his dress blues the last time she saw him. *(short pause)* Moira, I can't wait to get over there.

MOIRA I know. Thank God the Americans are in it now… there's bound to be a second front soon. Germany can't survive with the Russians on one side and us on the other.

ALLAN *(looking at his watch)* Four hours… train leaves at nine…. Look, Moira, I… we… Brantford's a long way off and I was wondering… will you write?

MOIRA *(sensing his real intentions)* Of course I will… you'll have another leave after Service Flying School. Don't *you* forget to write, okay?

ALLAN Sure… do you mind if we walk home?

MOIRA Four hours… you'll want to see your folks.

ALLAN Ya, but it's just… God, Moira, there are some things I want to say.

MOIRA Not here, okay? Let's walk.

They link arms. MOIRA and ALLAN address the audience, as if remembering the scene from the future:

While we walked, it started raining…

ALLAN I had the ring right in my pocket.

MOIRA I could tell he was crying. But he'd put out his hand and say, "It's sure coming down, eh?"

ALLAN For two weeks I'd planned how I'd ask her. But it wouldn't have been fair.

MOIRA I knew what he wanted to say.

ALLAN Her letter said, "I think about you constantly..."

MOIRA But I just kept seeing Norman's face, like we used to know him, not a care in the world...

ALLAN breaks away from MOIRA.

ALLAN Next leave, after Brantford, there'd be time to think, to get it right...

ALLAN takes his place back at his desk.

MOIRA *(to audience)* That's when I decided, if I was going to lose another man it wouldn't be sitting at home, hoping for a letter, dreading a telegram. There was a place for me somewhere.

Black.

When lights return, ALLAN and MOIRA are in their own spaces. He is writing from Service Flying Training School in Brantford. She is in Edmonton.

ALLAN *(writing)* March 20th, 1942

Brantford, Ontario.

Dear Moira,

Service Flying Training School has been a real eye-opener. We're working at a much higher intensity. Right now, I am training on Ansons. The Anson is a funny sort of aircraft that looks like a flying school bus, but is very forgiving to fly.

ALLAN, shaken, confides to the audience:

Williamson was making a blind approach under the hood. No one really knows what happened. He was coming in with no problem, textbook approach, when the starboard wing lifted. No apparent reason. Maybe he panicked, stopped believing the instruments. But the port tip caught the runway, the plane sort of bounced onto its nose, then started to cartwheel. It was like watching a ride at some macabre carnival. We all ran out to the crash, lifted the aircraft off its back. The fuel was leaking out. We were terrified. But no fire. Just Williamson, his neck broken, and the instructor, whose face was pretty badly smashed up, and who never stopped cursing a blue streak at us all the time we were lifting him out, his shin bone sticking right out through his trousers.

ALLAN nervously takes out a cigarette and lights it.

MOIRA takes out a cigarette and lights it.

MOIRA *(to the audience)* What's good for the gander is good for the goose. Dad says it's unladylike, so I chew a lot of Sen-Sen before I go home.

ALLAN *(butts out his cigarette, to audience)* I didn't used to smoke. But at I.T.S. our Flight Sergeant used to stop for smoke breaks. Anybody who didn't smoke would have to work while everybody else sat around. You don't have to hit me over the head with no ball-peen hammer.

But the worst part is the swearing. At Manning Depot, it was obvious that those who didn't pepper their vocabulary with every four-letter word weren't tough enough to make the grade.

I was shocked! Jesus, I was a lamb! But by the time of that first leave, I got off the train and there was Mom. I ran up and threw my arms around her.

"MOM!" I yelled, "Fuck, it's good to see you!"

He shakes his head in self-mocking disgust.

MOIRA *(writing)* Dear Allan,

I've taken a job up at Blatchford Field in Edmonton, where I can get near the war effort. There's going to be a lot of flyers there, so it's a way to stay close to you as well. My father's opinion is, "You should be at home helping your mother." He's afraid of what might happen to his little girl out on the base with all those dashing young airmen.

There are boys from all over the world.

(to herself) And God are they good-looking. I mean, some of them are. *(pause)* No. They all are. *(She laughs.)*

(*writing*) It's a long trip from the farm every morning. The train lands me downtown at seven-thirty, and then it's a dash to the streetcar which gets me to the airfield just before eight. My job is fun, and that's the main reason I'm doing it. Well, that and the money—thirty cents an hour! Get this—I'm driving a transport truck at the field. At first I thought that they weren't going to accept me because I'm a woman, but then I realised that more than half the drivers are. Say what you want, but the war has made some room for us, and I'm glad of it. I'm enjoying myself at work, at least now that the weather has gotten warmer, and very much enjoying the looks on people's faces when they ask me what I'm doing and I tell them I'm a truck driver.

ALLAN (*writing*) Dear Moira,

Well, well. The home front mustn't be a very safe place any more with you behind the wheel. But seriously, I'm not a bit surprised that you're doing what in peacetime would be considered a man's job…

MOIRA (*interrupts*) "What in peacetime…?" Just you wait.

ALLAN (*writing*) In the press, they're always trumpeting on about "Heroic Soviet women taking their places on the firing line." Sooner or later, I guess women will even be flying operationally. Though not in my lifetime, I hope.

MOIRA (*responds*) Dear Smarty pants,

For your information, I am enclosing a newspaper article from the *Journal*.

ALLAN (*reading the clipping*) "Recent aptitude tests have shown that women actually do better than men at jobs requiring manipulation dexterity."

(*to himself*) They faked the tests.

MOIRA (*writing*) June 13th, 1942

Dear Allan,

Maybe it was poor timing, but tonight at supper is when I told my parents that Dot and I are getting an apartment in Edmonton. I don't think my folks think much of

Dorothy, my dad made a few remarks that were very insinuating. Because Dot wears make-up, I suppose, or because she doesn't mind what she says to anybody. That's part of the reason I want to make this move. Our house is like a permanent funeral with Peter missing; Mom looks terrible, and Dad is taking it just as hard, though he tries not to show it.

She confides to the audience:

Dad feels guilty it's Peter and not him.

I think he's drinking an awful lot.

(writing) You must be getting near the end of Service Flying School. Any plans about your leave? I know a certain girl who'd love to go out dancing with you.

(She confides.) I'd like to do more than dance with him.

(writing) Can't wait to see you,

Love and a few kisses. A few hundred, that is.

The Royal Canadian Air Force (RCAF) March is heard. ALLAN puts on his dress tunic.

ALLAN *(writing)* Dear Moira,

I've been posted overseas! That's the good news. The bad news is, the posting is taking effect immediately. It's a rotten piece of luck for us, but the fact is, they're starting up a brand new Canadian Bomber Group, and I want to be in on the ground floor.

I'll let you know how it is in dear old Blighty. I'm sorry, Moira, I was looking forward to seeing you, but there's a war on.

Keep writing.

Love,

Allan.

ALLAN stands at attention, on parade. He salutes, proudly.

MOIRA reads his letter. It makes her furious. She crumples the paper and throws it away.

MOIRA "There's a war on!"

Pause. She picks the letter up. She sits.

(writing) Dear Allan,

I know how much it means to you to finally get into it.

I'd have liked to have seen you with your wings.

(to herself, angrily) But you had to rush into the goddamned war.

(writes, hiding her anger) I will miss you desperately. *(erases the last word)* I will miss you very much.

Love,

Moira.

Second Movement: Letters Overseas

ALLAN *(writing)* My first letter from overseas and I'm in ecstasy having received your four letters this morning...

MOIRA *(to audience)* ...four?

ALLAN *(writing)* I could tell there were a couple missing...

MOIRA ...more like a dozen...

ALLAN *(writing)* ...but things being the way they are, I'll just have to be patient. Some of the boys haven't received a thing, and they look so low when they see me poring over your letters again and again.

To top it off, a parcel arrived this morning from the T. Eaton Co. with wool socks, tooth powder, shaving soap, and a flashlight! I'm not sure what I'm allowed to tell you in letters, but if we mention anything specific, it'll get a quick clip from the censors...

MOIRA *(to herself)* "Loose lips sink ships."

ALLAN But here's a laugh for you! The ship we were on was packed with onions.

MOIRA *(directly to ALLAN)* Onions!

ALLAN *(directly to MOIRA)* Yes, onions! In every nook, onions! Under every bunk, onions! On the deck, between the depth charges, in the mess hall, underfoot everywhere, bags and bags of onions! But at least we were going too fast for any U-boats to catch us…

MOIRA *(writing)* I know… your sister wrote me a note. Being in signals, she had the information, and she wrote, "It's nice that Allan will get to see the late king's wife." *The Queen Mary*, of course! Fastest ship in the world!

ALLAN *(writing)* I wasn't supposed to say where I made that last phone call from, though.

MOIRA New York! She added at the bottom: "Have a Happy New Year!" underlining the "N" and the "Y". If it hadn't been October, I might not have caught on.

ALLAN It's "hurry up and wait" for us right now. Marching during the day and getting acquainted with what the English sarcastically call beer in the evenings. Don't worry, I'm taking it easy in that area. I'm eager to be posted. I'll have more news later, but all I can tell you right now is the food is terrible, the fellows are great, I'm sure to be active soon, and most of all, I love you with all my heart.

All my love,

Allan.

MOIRA *(writing)* November 11th, 1942

Dear Allan,

Today is Armistice Day. We all went down to the cenotaph this morning. Your dad was there, stumping along with the rest of the Great War vets. They are starting to look old, and the ranks are thinning. One wonders what they are all thinking as the news from Europe, Africa, Russia, and the South Pacific covers the headlines. Are they dying to be in it? Or do they feel relief. One thing I do know: that simple ceremony means so much to me, especially with Norman gone, and Peter, about whom we still have no word. I don't think anyone had a dry eye. For a country with so little military tradition, we sure have sacrificed a lot of our people.

(to herself) The women who were waiting for the boys to come back home after Vimy are still waiting for their life to start.

Not me.

ALLAN *(writing)* Number Three Personnel Receiving Centre is in Bournemouth, a former resort area on the south coast of England. Our digs are quite spiffy. We've taken over the hotels in the area.

MOIRA *(trying to make sense of ALLAN's visibly censored letter)* "There's little holiday spirit left, though."

ALLAN *(writing)* There's little holiday spirit left, though. The beaches have been mined and strewn with barbed wire waiting for the German invasion. Bofors guns are stationed every half-mile or so and manned by Home Guard, who take a few useless shots at any Jerries who stray too low going to and from raids…

MOIRA *(reading)* "We're earnestly resented by the locals."

ALLAN We're earnestly resented by the locals, who remember better days without us Canucks crowding their pubs and tennis courts.

MOIRA, puzzled, holds up ALLAN's letter, which is full of the holes the censor has cut in it.

MOIRA *(dryly)* He's in the silent service!

(writing) My dearest Allan,

Apartment life is quite interesting, especially with a roommate like Dot. She's what we call a real cut-up around here.

(to audience) I just wish she'd warn me when she's bringing a fellow home…

ALLAN *(writing)* My dearest Moira,

I'm still waiting for word on posting. In the meantime, we're often at loose ends to keep from getting bored to death.

(to audience) Getting drunk in the middle of the day was a new experience. Then it was going at it two days in a row. So was waking up with a head the size of the Macdonald Hotel and staggering to roll call. Luckily, they don't expect us to march anymore, so we're generally cut loose before noon.

(writing) I've done a couple of courses at a base near here. Some of the lucky dogs with over 500 hours have been posted. Guys like me with under 400 will have to wait our turn. Your neighbour, J.B., went yesterday.

MOIRA J.B... Jimmy Banes!

ALLAN *(writing)* I think about you constantly...

(to audience) ...especially when I see the shining faces of the English girls... birds, they call them here. They think us quite a novelty. We string them along with stories about shoot-outs against tribes of wild Indians on Jasper Avenue, and buffalo runs down Saskatchewan Drive. Jimmy Banes's favourite line is, "Some day, honey, you'll have to come to Alberta and tour my gopher ranch."

(writing) Dot sounds like a lot of fun...

(to himself) ...like a case of round heels and loose panties...

MOIRA *(writing)* I was home on the weekend. Mom and Dad are well, and asked about you. I wasn't able to get over to see your folks this trip...

(to herself) His dad is going to drive me nuts. He never fails to come up with something about the last war or Allan's certain death. Last time it was: "Well, Moira, dear, when all is said and done, I know he'll go clean." Just what the hell does he mean by that?

ALLAN *(writing)* Thanks for keeping in touch with Mom and Pop. I know this has been hard on them both...

(*to audience*) The old man is probably driving her nuts. I don't think he will ever get his mind past the Great War. I can see him holding forth about Vimy. It's always…

ALLAN & MOIRA (*together*) "Two steps out of the trench and the bastards blew it clean off!"

MOIRA (*to audience*) God, it's more than I can stand.

ALLAN (*to audience*) My first action turned out to be from a distance. Me and two of my new buddies, Johnny Gregoire and Bev Smillie, were out for a stroll along the beach one morning when we heard what sounded like fireworks. It turned out to be two Kraut Stukas who had the bad luck to be spotted by a couple of Spitfires. The Spits came down on them out of the sun; it was like sparrows on crows—a few bursts and the show was over. Only one of the Krauts got out. He opened his chute and we could see him picked up by coastal patrol a couple of minutes after he hit the drink. We ran almost two miles to get a look at the Jerry as he came off the boat.

What did he look like? Nothing special… just a chap… blond, kind of short, sturdy. No arrogance, no sneer or "Heil Hitler" as he passed us. He just looked at our tunics, for a second into our eyes. All I saw was relief. His war was over.

We walked back in silence. I was thinking: "Jesus Christ, there's a war on! Those bastards were shooting real bullets at one another…

When we reached the lobby, a fellow from down the hall yelled over, "Hey Staunton, did you hear about Jimmy Banes?"

I shook my head, figuring with Jimmy, it had to do with too much booze or skirt.

"He was killed a couple of days ago. Training flight. Burnt to a crisp."

ALLAN walks to his desk, begins composing a new letter.

Dear Mr. and Mrs. Banes,

I had the privilege of rooming with your son, Jimmy, when we arrived overseas…

MOIRA *(writing)* April 18th, 1943

Dearest Allan,

I've received a promotion! Eat your words, flyboy! I'm now on fuel trucks or what we call bowsers, but you probably know the term. I call it a promotion because it's a lot closer to the action. I'm fueling up mostly trainers—Harvards, Ansons, and the odd Tiger Moth…

ALLAN *(writing)* Dearest Moira,

Sorry I haven't written sooner. I've been through a lot of changes lately and been kept busy with my training. I can't tell you where I'm based, or even what kind of airplane I'm now flying. Suffice to say that the plane is not from the house of York, if you read your Shakespeare.

MOIRA *(to herself)* Not from the house of York… Lancaster! He's flying Lancasters?

(writing) I dropped in on the Feniaks last weekend. They asked about you. They took me up to Norman's room and it would bring you to tears to see how Mrs. Feniak has kept it as if Norman was still in high school and expected home any moment for lunch. By the look Chester gave me I could tell he was distressed. I hope she gets on with things soon.

ALLAN *(continues)* Always happy to receive your letters. News from home is swell, even if it's just about how many eggs your mother picked on Saturday.

Thanks loads for the cigs. Believe me, nine hundred a month isn't too many.

The enclosed snap is of our crew. I've written their names on the back and where they're from. The guy with the

Stetson is our Wireless Air Gunner, "Cowboy." He's always bragging about how many Krauts he's going to shoot down… *(short pause)* The short guy on the left, Roy Toane, was our rear gunner. He isn't with us anymore.

Was at the pub last night, we're not flying, due to a… little mishap. After our next op, we're due to go on leave for a while, and I'm going to take the train down to London, poke about in the big city and see Saint Paul's and all that.

I think of Norman often.

Much love…

(to audience) My first op on a Lancaster last night. Scotty gets up beside me in the cockpit. I look at him: "Scotty, do you know how to start one of these fucking things?" "Don't yooou?" he asks. "Hell no," I tell him. When I did my checkout, the training officer landed the goddamned thing and I got in while it was still running. We did a few circuits and bumps, and then he got out and said, "Looks like you've got it, off you go."

So Scotty and I, our first operational flight, we don't know how to start the goddamn airplane. We figured it out eventually, and got off okay. But does that plane fly, like a fighter after the Hallybag and the Wimpy.

Unfortunately, we had a brush with Jerry over the target.

A Folke Wolf 190 caught up to us after we had released our bombs. The first I knew that we'd been attacked was when I noticed she was yawing to port, and then the rear turret fired. When Roy didn't talk to us, our mid-upper, Sandy Smith, crawled back to the rear turret and tried to force the door. He couldn't. The kite was shot up badly, I had no port rudder control. We got down all right using a series of right-hand turns, which the controller wasn't pleased about, but a kite in one piece, even full of holes, is better than a mess on his runway, I guess.

As we shut down, Sandy jumped out and hurried round the back with the erks. What a mess. The Perspex was shattered. Roy was lying in a pool of blood, unconscious, but he came to as we were lifting him out of the turret. His left eye was simply dangling from the side of his face. I don't know how he was enduring the pain. I guess you just do.

The odd thing is, Roy managed to shoot the guy down. On his first pass, the German was apparently just trying to knock out the rear gunner. I suppose he thought he'd succeeded, and seeing the turret, you could see why. For one thing, Roy's guns were jammed in one position. So the Kraut, thinking he'd have all night to chop us up, flew right past Roy's gun-sight, and Roy pulled the trigger. Said he could see the tracer flying right into Jerry's cockpit. The 190 rolled over and fell away, then Roy blacked out.

They say they may be able to save most of the vision in the other eye, but they'll have to sort of rebuild the left side of his face.

We'll be assigned a new tail gunner in a day or two.

MOIRA (*writing*) July 6th, 1943

You won't believe it! The old hometown just went over 100,000! Of course it's all the Americans that have moved in to help build the highway to Alaska.

The whole city has a new look. A lot of their money has been put into rinks, tennis courts and the like, and renovating some older buildings, like the Jesuit College. I can't wait to go to one of those new hamburger emporiums with you.

But you sure can't mistake the Yankees. They don't seem to go anywhere without making some sort of noise. Maybe it's their cars, their swagger, their pockets full of money, but mostly it's the attitude they have that we should all be very grateful they're here.

Your dad says it was the same in 1917 when they landed in France. Mayor LaGuardia of New York visited in July and the *Bulletin* reported that he said Edmonton was "a most attractive city… from the air." Imagine the nerve!

(to audience) Dot just loves the Yanks. She says Huck Finn's a hell of a lot more fun than Oliver Twist. I didn't even know Dot read.

(writing) Your folks invited me to picnic with them last week, and a number of their troops had taken over most of Borden Park. I can't say I was impressed with their behaviour.

(to audience) …or the behaviour of some of the local girls who hung on them like scarves. But there really is something about young men in uniform. They kept looking over my way, I'm sure because they feel that any unattached woman is fair game.

"Jesus Christ on skis," Dot tells me, "you don't know what you're missing, honey!" What she doesn't know is that I get to chat up boys from almost anyplace over at the field. I'm usually dressed in coveralls, but that doesn't stop them from leaning out of their jeeps to see what they can see. The Yanks are bad, but nothing like the Aussies.

ALLAN *(writing)* September 28th, 1943

Dear Moira,

When you mentioned the Yanks working at home in your last letter, you probably heard me laugh right over the Atlantic. You ought to see them here.

Up until now, we've kind of had the run of the place. The Brits accepted us as their poor cousins from the colonies. The Americans of the United States Army Air Force, known as the 8th, act like they own the place. They get paid about twice what we Canadians do, and about three times what the Brits do.

There's always a gang of them bellied up to the bar, throwing five-pound notes around and making fun of everything English.

But we get our own back sometimes. They wear a lot of medals on their tunics, which by the way are pink, of all colours. Anyhow we have a guy in our squadron, ex-Mountie, who likes to approach some Yank in a bar and gaze with mock-awe at the victim's chest and say, "Gosh, look at that beautiful medal. What'd you get that for, eating your breakfast?

(to himself) What really bothers me is that the sons of bitches travel in hordes, so you're sitting in some pub chatting up a bird and thinking you're making progress, when about fifty of them will come in and take the place over. Right away the bird knows that she can graduate from bitter to Scotch, and you know you've either got to talk faster, or dig deeper.

ALLAN suddenly feels the cold. He puts on his tunic, his battle-dress, and his greatcoat. He's still cold.

(writing) Your package arrived in time for Christmas. A welcome sight, and thanks for wrapping it so well. It keeps the contents out of "enemy" hands.

MOIRA *(writing)* So glad to hear my parcel arrived. The cigarettes aren't hard to get, but finding that prepared chocolate was a stroke of luck.

(to audience) Dot picks it up from one of her Yankee boyfriends. I don't want to know the details.

(writing) I surprised Mom and Dad by bringing Dot home for Christmas dinner. I think they expected the worst, but believe it or not, she brightened the place up, just what the doctor ordered. After dinner she traded farming stories with Dad, and then got everyone into a singsong at the piano. When she sang "I Wonder Who's Kissing Her Now," you could have knocked Mom and Dad over with a feather. They'd really taken a liking to her by the time we left.

(to audience) We didn't want to miss the dance.

ALLAN *(writing)* The prepared chocolate is "bang-on" as they say here. Just add water and mix. A real hit with the guys! If you ever find more…

MOIRA *(calling offstage)* Dottie! Who's on for tonight? *(to herself)* Oh, Christ, I can't believe I said that.

ALLAN *(writing)* The five-day I wangled in early December was great! I took in the sights of Edinburgh.

(to audience) Queen Street! Eight blocks of pubs that do us more damage than the Luftwaffe ever could. The legend is that no one has ever had a drink in every pub and lived to tell the tale. I tried. I failed. But it was an historic piss-up. A ten-hour blur, a League of Nations of laughing, singing, slap-on-the-back, hail fellows well met, the shoulder flashes announcing Brits, Canucks, Yanks, Norwegians, Free French, Poles…

I started at one end with my right pocket full of half crowns. A shilling a beer, a shilling a gin, the change going into my left, so I was listing badly to port by the time I admitted defeat. It was in a pub where a Canadian artillery sergeant had taken over the piano, and we settled in to endless choruses of…

ALLAN sings ditties from the following songs, in various accents: "Don't Sit Under the Apple Tree," "Good Night Irene," "Red River Valley," and especially "Rum and Coca-Cola."

He suddenly feels ill.

How I ended up in the hostel, face-down on my pillow, I'll credit to that angel who hovers over sweethearts, fools, and drunks.

(writing) I'm not suffering from lack of things, and I know you are making sacrifices at home, too.

MOIRA *(to audience)* Sugar was just cut from three-quarters to half a pound a week, tea and coffee by half, and meat… well, I'm lucky Mom and Dad are on the farm. Canning season was hard on Mom last year, so Dad butchered a bull and I traded meat to some of the girls for their sugar rations. The sign in the store says: "Loyal citizens do not hoard." What are they going to do, shoot me?

Third Movement: Lies and Valentines

MOIRA *(writing)* February 14th, 1944

Dear Allan,

I'm so glad about the good news from the South Pacific. The Americans are really giving it to the Japanese, and with any hope, there will soon be a new front. The really big news, though, is that it's just Valentine's Day, and so I'm sending you this by way of a Valentine, and asking, "will you be mine?"

(re-reading) "Will you be mine…?" Jesus.

(erasing, then writing) Your letter certainly perked up my spirits, just what I needed as I was home on the weekend and made the rounds to see your parents and then over to the Feniaks. Your mom and dad were fine, except that your dad complained bitterly about rationing, somehow wondering aloud why a veteran of the Great War had to make sacrifices again.

ALLAN *(writing)* Dear Moira,

Well, another year passes, and we're still at it. It seems we've been going at this forever, I really don't know how the Krauts can keep it up, fighting a war on three fronts, because they are, whatever the papers say.

I'm in London, managed to wangle a 3-day leave. As I write to you, I'm just preparing to go out for another night on the town, would you believe it? "Where to?" some conductor will ask. "Piccadilly," I'll say, just like I was saying, "Jasper and First." Still haven't been in St. Paul's, but I've been past it twice a day. Leave ends tomorrow, and I'm attending a little party tonight put on at the home of one of the foreign diplomats, one of the perks we get for being shot at."

(to audience) She had a strange manner about her, and I don't just mean about her accent. As though all the time she spent with me she was really half thinking of other things.

She is Polish, and she speaks with a heavy Slavic rumble. Very alluring. But that didn't stop this Brit colonel from sidling up to me and whispering, "Nice, but a bit colourful, what?" I didn't know what the hell he was talking about. "Jewish," he says.

The CO introduced me and told her I was from Western Canada. "I suppose you, how you call it, lasso leetle beefs?" she says. I'm trying to be clever, I say, "No ma'am, I don't lasso little beefs, I just put up with them from the crew."

Which just goes to show you should never crack jokes with foreigners. "Mr. Cowboy," she says, "I want you should dance with me tonight." So I did. It was very good. We parted at the end of the night, but she gave me her address.

MOIRA *(writing)* There was a big dance out at the field last night, everyone was there. I didn't want to go, but Dot convinced me. You've got to meet her, she's as crazy as a bedbug. Mart Kenny's band was playing—who says we're making sacrifices? I did have one or two drinks, but nothing untoward happened.

Oh I must tell you about the nice Norwegian pilot I met. He came up to me suddenly and explained in his broken English that I reminded him of his sweetheart back home.

(to herself, confessional) Ingvar Norqvist. He's a Norwegian. Very tall, and blond. He flies. He's in training on the base. He's onto Harvards now. He speaks English almost like an Englishman. Those long vowels. *(imitating)* "How do you do?"

He escaped Norway in 1940, skiing out part of the way, and then he and three friends took a small open boat into the North Sea. He was eighteen at the time. His life is like a novel. They killed his brother. *(beat)* He is so sad.

Dot introduced us at the dance. She is terrible. "Ingvar, this is my friend Moira. Did you know Moira means fate in Greek?" With a terrible glinting smile at me.

We danced. He is awkward, doesn't have a feel for swing at all. I had to teach him. He held me very close. He needs something. So do I…

I think I'm in love.

ALLAN *(writing)* Dear Moira,

This last leave spent in London one of the most interesting times I've had since coming over.

(to audience) I spent the whole thing in her apartment. We screwed like maniacs.

MOIRA *(writing)* "Work at the base is hum-drum. Dot says hello."

(to audience) Dot is pregnant.

ALLAN *(writing)* London is all blacked out of course, so at night there's an almost eerie darkness on the streets, and people walk around like ghosts, with their voices low, as though the Germans could hear them.

(to audience) Walking home you can hear all the pros and the tarts, also known as Piccadilly Commandos, in the doorways. Christ, I swear half this city is gone completely nymphomaniac, they do it in doorways, up alleys, they'd use the phone booths if they thought they'd fit.

MOIRA *(writing)* I went out to a big V-bond party with some friends.

(to audience) I left with Ingvar. We siphoned some gas from my truck. We drove out to Cooking Lake. It was… very romantic.

ALLAN & MOIRA *(together, to audience)* Why do all of his/her letters sound so phony?

ALLAN *(writing)* Of course, London isn't in anything like the danger it was in during the real blitz, but they're taking no chances, and the squareheads still make the occasional raid to prove their bomber forces are still in it. Even though they're not, of course, ha, ha, compared to what we're doing to them. You can't imagine what it's like, from twenty-five thousand feet, watching a city get pulverised by a thousand-bomber raid. And I don't cry for the Krauts. They asked for it, and we're giving it to them.

I wanted to visit St. Paul's as I told you, on the last leave, but once again it seemed damn hard to get around to it. The war… has done funny things to people, me included.

MOIRA *(to audience)* I wrestle with it constantly… my shame and my desire. Even though Allan doesn't deserve this, I do…

(writing) You might be interested to know that I'm now in charge of transport operations for the entire field. My responsibilities include allocation, scheduling, filling in for sick drivers when the need arises. Yesterday, the base CO told me I was doing an excellent job. I like working, and I like the money it brings.

The war… has changed this little city very much. I wonder if you'd recognise it.

ALLAN *(writing)* I wonder if you'd recognise me.

ALLAN & MOIRA *(together)* If I should appear to have changed when next we meet, please don't be too shocked.

MOIRA *(to herself)* Oh, drat it all! *(erases her last remark)*

ALLAN *(to himself)* Fuck. *(erases his last remark)*

ALLAN & MOIRA *(together)* Well, I'll close,

Love,

Allan/Moira

ALLAN *(to himself)* People don't know what it's like to go into hell one night and be pissed on champagne the next. They don't know how insane it is, how fucking funny, how… extreme. My 29th op tonight. Hanover. If I live, I'm going to tell the CO to put me up for another thirty. Then a fortnight in London. I'm going to stay drunk. And stay with her.

MOIRA *(tries to write a "Dear John" letter)* Dear Allan,

I have not received a letter from you for several weeks now. I don't know what this means, but I pray to God that it doesn't mean you're injured or ki– missing. I have to tell you that I have been remiss in writing because…

(to audience) Because why? Because everything has changed in our little lives. Because I've been working at my own job, a difficult, responsible job. Because everything is so much more important than one individual. Because I can't stand knowing whether or not you're dead at the moment I'm writing these letters.

(writing) I've been remiss in writing because… I've been doing a great many other things. And because I've been doing some other dating. I recently met a Norwegian pilot who's in the Commonwealth Air Training Plan here. He's going to be finished soon, and then he will be leaving, posted somewhere in Europe. He is a very nice fellow, Allan, and I…

I can't write this.

She crumples up the unfinished letter, throws it away.

Fourth Movement: On Ops

ALLAN *(to the audience)* Dusk falls. The nervous lorry ride out to dispersal. Our Lanc, D for Dumbo, is way out at the end of the runway, so we're last to get off the truck. Charlie goes and pisses against the rear wheel. We used to bug him about it, ask him why he didn't wait till we were all in the aircraft so we wouldn't tread in it. Now, after twenty-nine ops with only one casualty, nobody bugs him any more.

The flight engineer and I go round the kite and check the tire pressure, the oleos, the control surfaces and cables. Every now and then you hear about some poor bastard who didn't take off his rudder or elevator locks. Smoke and tar at the end of the runway.

When I first saw the Lanc I thought she was kind of ugly. Like a great big insect with bulbous protrusions all over her. But when you see her from some angles. From behind, quarter-view, you see how beautiful those fat wings are, even the huge tail surfaces, you can feel the power of her design, the perfect utility of what she was designed to do. And what she was designed to do is hanging in the bomb bay. Thousand pounders to break things apart, gas and water mains, then incendiaries to set the whole thing on fire. And four big beautiful Merlins to bring you back safe.

I pat the left rudder, then the right, pound on the back of the rear turret, and then walk once clockwise completely around the plane. Don't ask me why, I just do it. Then I get in. Climbing up to the cockpit over the main spar isn't easy with all your kit. The guys try not to think about what it would be like to try to get to the rear exit with the aircraft hit and spinning in the dark. I strap myself in, plug in the oxygen, usually pull a few deep breaths to clear the head. We check oxygen supply and intercom, and I ask everybody to report standing by. When I've finished the cockpit check, I signal the ground crew: Start 'em!

The noise of airplane engines, growing in volume, as the lights fade on ALLAN, suspended like a statue of a man, going forward to an uncertain future.

ACT II

ALLAN is in his airplane.

ALLAN *(shouting the first words)* START EM!

The noise of the engines begins. It continues, all the way till the end of this speech.

Four engines, port to starboard. Set revs for 1000 rpm, let 'em warm up, then check pitch control for each engine at 2800, throttle back to plus six thrust and check mag drop.

We taxi out, feeling the low bounce of the wheels carrying the heavy weight of the bomb load. Control the speed with the handbrake, steer with the outer engines. Before turning onto the runway, final runup check: trim, revs, flaps, mag drop, pressure. Okay. Onto the runway. There's a flare from the hut. All right, boys? This is it. Line her up, apply the brakes and give her all four throttles. I wave the engineer away, I'll do this one myself. The noise builds, unbelievable nearly, the Merlins howling. She's bucking to move. I let off the brakes and she begins to roll, slow and lumbering at first, but gathering speed rapidly. Christ, the torque is pulling us to starboard, I roll back the port outer throttle and she corrects herself. The tail wheel lifts off and I have some control with the rudder now. Quick glance at the airspeed. 85… 90. She gently lifts her wheels off the deck and the bumping stops. I hold her low to get the ground effect, build up airspeed. Pull up the nose, now, she wants to fly, up she climbs at 165 knots. What a feeling. God.

The ground disappears rapidly now, it's nearly dusk. We climb to set course altitude, joining the first off and waiting for the others. Check the time. Right. Steer one zero five by the gyro. We're on our way. Now the routine starts. Nav? ETA to turning point, please. Two hours, twenty minutes. We're gradually climbing to tonight's bombing height, 23,000. I fiddle with the trim, feel the urge to piss, suppress it, try to relax.

First crisis, flak from the Dutch coast. Jerry never fails to get a shot at us. We're flying over eight-tenths cloud and the bastards are still uncannily accurate. They have radar control, and their predictors work very well. I begin to weave gently, maybe a useless exercise. At least it's something. For chrissake keep an eye out, guys. Our biggest danger is running into one of our own kites.

We reach the turning point over Arnheim and try to fool the Germans by making a turn onto our main target. As if Jerry is fooled. Christ there's eight hundred bombers in the stream, Jerry isn't stupid, he knows exactly where we're headed. Into the fucking Ruhr valley again. Into the valley of death. There's a goddamn garden party waiting for us. The searchlights form a reception line. Security is now a joke. You wait for one of the blue lights to cone you. The flak is all over the sky now. A burst close enough that I swear I can hear it over the engines, and the mid-upper reports that he can hear the shrapnel against the fuselage. I'm fighting the control column now, the turbulence from all the explosions. There's enough light that we can catch occasional silhouettes from the rest of the bomber stream.

O Christ, they've found us with the blue light. God, the cockpit lights up like somebody was using a blowtorch in here. Jesus, the rest of the lights will cone me in a second, and then we're dead. Dive straight into the light, hard port rudder, full left aileron. We're going downhill fast, 22 thousand, 21, 20, 19, 18. The light is still incredibly bright, I can't see a fucking thing. Somebody is screaming into the intercom. Shut up, you asshole, SHUT UP! I jink left, then right… I lose the bastard! But now I'm diving nearly out of control, airspeed exceeding 325, Jesus, with a full load of bombs. Have to haul her out. Pull off the power, and I'm hauling back with all my strength. It's like wrestling an elephant. The trim! I roll it back all the way. Down to three thousand feet, and the nose is just starting to come up.

Holy Christ, we're not going to make it. We're below the surrounding hills! Something inside my brain shuts down. I'm not aware of any fear, anywhere, just me and this control column. Pull!

The plane starts to come out of the dive, and I'm pressed down into my seat by the G-force. The blood is draining out of my head, I'm half-dizzy. We are going to make it, we are going to make it. The nose comes up at last, I can hear something creaking. God bless the people that built this airplane!

God, we're starting to climb up! We need power: I run the throttles up. Two of the Merlins roar, one coughs, one chokes completely. Jesus H Christ. Jock, get that port inner started again! Somebody's mumbling in my headset, Jesus it's Jimmy in the tail turret, he's saying Hail Marys, the Catholic sonovabitch. Jimmy, shut up for chrissake.

Jock has the engines all going now and we're climbing. Give me a course to target, Ed. No, I'm not going to jettison and go home, we won't even get credit for this raid. How will they know? *I'll know.* Besides, there's the cameras. We'll join the bomber stream late and drop from twenty thousand. George, bring that bottle up here, will you, I have to piss something terrible.

As we approach Essen, there's no doubt about the location of the target. The whole horizon is one big conflagration, Christ, we're pounding the hell out of it tonight. The flak is terrible. Two miles to port, there's a flame in the sky where someone has an engine on fire. The fireball is gradually descending. Jesus Christ, boys, get out before it goes. I hope to God it's nobody I know. Flak everywhere, occasionally you can see tracer.

The bomb aimer takes control of the aircraft. All I have to do is the only thing every nerve ending is screaming at me not to do: fly straight and level and give the bastards a perfect target. I slump down in my seat, so I can't see, and fly blind where the bomb aimer wants me. Charlie is very good. He's leaning over his sights in the nose, talking calm and low. I hold her steady as I can. Open bomb doors! Bombs away! The aircraft lurches upward, freed of five tons weight. We have to hold course for another two minutes for the cameras. I've got the wind up seriously now, the flak gunners seem to be getting our range. Fifteen seconds more and we'll turn to port and dive away from this shit.

O CHRIST we've been hit. Like a giant bashed us with an almighty hammer. ENGINEER WHAT'S GOING ON. Everyone report. Oh Christ it's Sandy in the mid-upper, he's caught some flak, SHUT UP GODDAMN YOU STOP SCREAMING. Something is vibrating like crazy, my hands are being nearly shaken off the yoke, and now I see the flame licking out of the starboard inner HIT THE FIRE EXTINGUISHER and feather SHIT the hydraulics have packed it in, the goddamn prop can't be feathered and we're yawing to starboard. What am I thinking? Dive starboard… the engine fire is like a beacon to the fighters. I crank the column over, mush through a 30 degree turn and start praying she doesn't spiral on me with God knows what damage to the control surfaces. But she comes out flat and level oh you beautiful bird. I trim the rudder to keep us flying straight against the pull of the extra port engine. GIVE ME A COURSE, Ed, tell me how to go home, straight home. God knows how much fuel we've lost or how much we need. I settle in for two and a half hours of being shaken by this wounded airplane. Jock has stopped the fuel flow to the dead engine, and is figuring out how to juggle his reserves. The mid is mercifully not on intercom now, he's been given morphine and is lying over the main spar.

Now the battle of nerves, flying a wounded kite all the way home, the Krauts can track you on radar, they know you're travelling slow, and will have some speed merchant in a Mess 410 after you. Your watch becomes your enemy, you keep looking at it occasionally expecting half-hours to have passed and discovering that only minutes have.

After an hour you want to smoke, you want to sleep. Your attention wanders. I talk to the guys every few minutes, get them to check in, get them to keep watching. This is the time of awful danger, you need to close your eyes, you think it's over. The first glimmerings of light on the horizon behind you. Perfect cover for the fighters coming up from below. I'm scanning the sky for cloudbanks to duck into if we're attacked. Of course, for once, the weather is ideal.

North Sea now, no flak opposition on the coast, I wonder why. Don't let us into that terrible cold sea. But the Merlins purr. We cross the coast. My left leg is shaking on the rudder. Crash positions, boys! We're given a circuit, of course the air is full of Lancs trying to get down. I tell them we've got wounded, and they put us first. Next crisis: the landing gear. Jock and I look at each other, cross fingers, select "down." We get greens, thank Christ. The flare path. Set her down, fly her on, God knows what speed she'll stall at with this damage, keep it over a hundred. We bounce once, twice, the port outer quits suddenly, we swing left. Images of the ambulance racing along the runway, the fire wagon. We leave the tarmac, the wheels dig into the grass, we slow down, slew sideways, the right tire explodes, this is all happening in slow motion, the oleo collapses, the wing digs in, I'm thrown left against the windows. We stop spinning. I reach over and shut the engines down. We're home.

The lights go down on the image of ALLAN, slumped in his chair. On the other side of the stage, MOIRA, in silhouette, takes off her blouse. She gestures to someone to be quiet. She lights a cigarette, and laughs. She sighs.

Black.

Fifth Movement: Fibre, Moral and Immoral

MOIRA and ALLAN, writing.

MOIRA June 7th, 1944.

Dear Allan…

ALLAN Dear Moira…

MOIRA Oh, God, what great news about the invasion of France…

ALLAN I have looked at a page of history. The second front has finally been opened on the beaches of Normandy…

MOIRA We have lived with constant dread about the outcome of the war for three and a half years, but at last we can feel that there is some end in sight, and that our side is going to win.

ALLAN We flew three raids yesterday, bombing German positions… at least we hope they were German positions, and the incredible array of ships, tanks and men was beyond imagination.

MOIRA Everyone home was glued to the radio as Lorne Green read the news from the front. It is said that the Canadians are at the forefront of some of the fighting.

ALLAN Everything was under a cloud of explosives, shellfire, and smoke from the ships trying to cover the men in the landing craft, but you could see, here and there, groups of men running up the beach, some of them collapsing like little tin soldiers…

MOIRA Mother says we ought to pray for them, but I can't…

ALLAN Canada has a whole division at Juno beach, and our guys have done well, I understand. We're not in their good books, though…

MOIRA My own faith in God has been so shaken by the events of this war, I can't bring myself to pray.

ALLAN One of our crews was ordered to fly in and drop antipersonnel bombs on some water tower, and after they finished their drop, they flew over a second water tower where the Germans actually were…

MOIRA Gordon Priggit, Don Howard, John McConnogh, Jimmy Banes, Norman Feniak…

ALLAN The guys feel sick, but what can you do?

MOIRA I don't know who to be mad at. The Nazis are just indistinct characters in funny helmets. I'm mad at Prime Minister King, who's always trying to get his picture taken with Roosevelt and Churchill. And I look at all those pictures of guns and tanks and planes, and I think, those things aren't made for free, someone's getting profit out of them. And I wonder, if no one was making any money out of this war, would it have been going on so long?

She silently re-reads what she has written, then crumples it up. She starts again.

Dear Allan,

Oh, God, what great news about the invasion of France. At last, we can feel that there is some end in sight, and that our side is going to win…

ALLAN *(writing)* Dear Moira,

I am writing to everyone back in Canada, to you, and to my folks and friends, to let you know that I will not be coming home within the foreseeable future. I have finished my first tour of duty…

MOIRA *(reading)* His *first* tour of duty?

ALLAN *(writing)* …and I have volunteered for a second tour. I will probably be promoted, but I can't say that this is my motive. To tell you the truth, I can't exactly say why I want to stay over here. I wish I could tell you it was for patriotic reasons, but it's not.

(to himself) When I think about getting off the train in Edmonton, Alberta, and facing all those people. People who think that we're heroes. Last week, over Dortmund,

we saw three of our kites go for a Burton in one minute. All flamers. Smitty, our Wireless Air Gunner, starts singing "it could happen to you, it could happen to you," and we're all nearly out of control. I think Charlie was on the verge of shooting him. I screamed at him to shut up, finally somebody hit him. When we got back, everyone hopped on the truck, but no Smitty. He wouldn't get out of the aircraft. I thought he was embarrassed, so I went back into the plane to get him. "Come on, Smitty," I told him, "nobody's going to blame you." He started crying. "I can't get onto that truck with them, Skipper," he says, "you see, I've shit myself, and I stink to high heaven."

MOIRA (*writing*) Dear Allan,

The news of the D-Day invasion kept us glued to the radio here for weeks. I have been following the tracing of the battle lines on my European Atlas, at least as far as can be made out from the news broadcasts. The other day I was at The Bay looking for some shoes, and I heard two of the salespeople refer to our troops in Italy as the D-Day slackers. Can you imagine?

(*to audience*) The invasion is driving Ingvar out of his mind. He can't wait to be posted over there. When he talks about the Germans, his eyes turn pale, and if anyone even mentions Quisling, he stomps out of the room.

He is bound to be posted soon. What in God's name will happen if Ingvar is still here when Allan comes home?

ALLAN (*writing*) Dearest Moira,

I must tell you about a funny experience that happened to me at a party in London several months ago. At the party I met a Polish woman, who had apparently once been very rich in her own country, but all her family's money was confiscated because they're Jewish. She asked me if I lassoes beefs, and I told her I didn't lasso any beefs, but that I'd been putting up with some from the crew, which I thought was kind of smart, but she didn't get the joke at all. Anyway, I thought it was kind of funny.

He looks up. He crumples the letter, discards it.

(to audience) The hell of being CB'd is not being able to get away… to get to London… her apartment… to lose myself in clean sheets… the smell of the perfume in her hair.

The worst of it is too much time to think… about how you're gonna get it… about that shell fragment grazing your ear from behind and knocking the compass off your panel… about the 109 pilot waving as he flew by your nose too low on petrol or ammo to make another pass… and you wonder what would've happened if you'd lifted off the tarmac half a second earlier, or if the armourers had squeezed one more 500-pounder into your bay, or if the 109 hadn't used up his ammo ripping the shit out of another kite.

MOIRA *(to audience)* I get a little sick of them hanging around me when Ingvar isn't around. I should have known there'd be some who figure they can step in and take his place… when I reject them, they look at me like I'm diseased… piss on them.

ALLAN *(to audience)* Oh, Bomber Command is real good with statistics. What they give us is big numbers of Kraut night fighters shot down and low ones on how many of our kites have gone for the chop. Shit, even those of us who're only sober half the time can figure it out. An air crew that lasts more than ten ops is pushing the odds.

And Christ, if we'd destroyed as much of Germany as Harris claims, there'd be nothing left but a huge hole from the Rhine to Berlin.

MOIRA Even the dances don't seem so glamorous any more… those fresh young faces that once fascinated me… now they're just guys you'll never see again after six weeks.

ALLAN I just hope it's quick… Like R-Robert over Stuttgart, floating along fifty yards off my starboard wing…. A kite one second… ka fuckin boom… garbage the next.

MOIRA It really gets me when these guys who've been in Canada since '39 strut up with their brass all polished and expect you to lift your skirt. Christ, I've got to clean up my mouth. I still see Dot once in a while. God, the joys of motherhood. She came to a couple of dances afterwards, but the news was out.

ALLAN I just don't want to have the North Sea rushing into my face, or a stray shell winging me, taking the controls out of my hands with six other guys depending on me.

MOIRA *(reading)* "Allied airmen who parachuted into three unnamed places in central Germany Monday were killed by agitated people." Oh, Allan…

ALLAN …or having to bail out… that's the worst. Who knows what happened to Norman. Even if he did get out of his kite, he could've ended up hanging in some town square for all we know. I keep having this dream, a dream that even a bellyful of gin can't drown. I'm falling into the blackest of holes when above me my chute opens… FOOMP… I look up… there's no chute… it's my first flying instructor, screaming at me… "Incompetent asshole! You screwed up again!" …I look down and in the distance I see D-Dumbo hit the deck in a ball of flame. My crew's in that fire… I can hear them screaming…. Shit, my intercom's still on! I'm floating down… there's a crowd of people… they're reaching for me… I wake up…

MOIRA We've got Paris now. You'd think they could let up on the German cities. It's got to be almost over. Oh, to lose you now…

ALLAN "Cowboy" used to brag that he'd hidden his asthma from the M.O. when he'd enlisted. Last month they caught him with his face in a hole in his mattress. He was pounding on it, inhaling the dust till he was coughing blood. He's on his way home with L.M.F. across his discharge: Lack of Moral Fibre…

But you look around and see the rest of them coping. You drown the hours in the mess, sing the songs, tell the stories, and wait… eventually you coax her into the air and head for the Fatherland.

MOIRA *(writing)* Dear Allan: The news from the front gets better day by day. Our boys in Holland, the Yanks across the Rhine, the Russians pushing to Berlin.

ALLAN *(writing)* Sorry to have forgotten your mother's birthday. Please give her my best. *(pause, then)* Do you remember Elmer Swanson from school?

MOIRA *(to herself)* The Air Training program officially closed on the 31st, so it looks like I'll be back on Civvie Street soon.

ALLAN I ran into him in London. He was in the Commandos from D-Day on and with the first Canadians over the Rhine. They came upon one of those German internment camps at a place called Bergen-Belsen. It had been used for Jews and anyone else the Nazis didn't feel was suited to the master race.

MOIRA *(writing)* You may have some idea of the extent of the Training Plan. With it closing, we will suddenly find ourselves in a little provincial backwater again. My friend Ingvar, a Norwegian flyer that I have mentioned in another letter, is going to be posted any day now.

ALLAN *(writing)* The few living were skeletons. The rest… thousands… were piled up like firewood. The survivors who knew English told of slave labour, torture, summary executions on the whim of the SS…

Believe me, you don't want to hear the rest.

MOIRA *(to audience)* And I will be left here, watching a small yellow airplane fly into the sun.

Sixth Movement: Finding a Way Home

ALLAN *(writing)* Dear Moira,

I'm kind of curious about what you're up to. I haven't heard from you for a while, and I'm wondering about this Norwegian flyer you've mentioned. Maybe I shouldn't write this, but I can't help but be curious. Write me a letter when you feel like it. It's been a strange time.

I probably won't be able to mail this for a while, security reasons. But I'm curious.

Affectionately yours,

Allan.

MOIRA *(thinking aloud)* "Affectionately yours?" *(pause)* He knows.

(writing) Dear Allan,

I received your letter today several weeks after it was written, and I can't make out the postmark. I wrote you about my pleasure on hearing that the end is at last in sight. I have to tell you that I don't know what you mean to imply with your remarks about Norwegian flyers, but I just want you to start considering what kind of pot you have on to boil before you start calling the kettle black.

ALLAN *(reading this, mutters)* She knows.

MOIRA *(writing)* March 8th, 1945

Dear Allan,

I have been procrastinating about writing this letter for several weeks. I feel cheap and cowardly about it, but I can't change the facts. For several months, I was seeing a young man who was with the BCATP here. His name is Ingvar Norqvist. He is a brave decent person and at this point I feel he's been more decent than me.

(to audience) He was like some Norse god. He was quiet and confident, and sometimes he flashed with anger. He had seen too much. Once, he told me what happened the day they escaped Norway. Sneaking house-to-house in the dark, and climbing down the city walls onto the frozen lake. The barking of the dogs, and the wild pursuit. Seeing his own brother collapse, shot dead, right beside him…

He was so hurt, so tender. So full of grim purpose. They all knew. No doubt about it. The times we left the dances early. The looks I asked him to conceal. He asked me to be strong. I pretended I was, and I became what I pretended. My mother fears what's happened, but she knows she has no authority now to forbid anything. I guess I could tell her that I'm still technically a virgin, but that would be getting pretty technical. *(laughs)* My father says nothing, but somehow I think he understands.

On the train platform, we didn't even kiss. It was his choice, he didn't want to compromise me. To tell the truth, it was so much like a scene from "Casablanca" that I wasn't absolutely sure we weren't in the movies. I wished him luck, and told him… I know it sounds corny, but I told him I hoped Norway would soon be free. He didn't take it as a joke. He gave me a parting gift: I don't know where he found it.

She holds up a book.

The Odyssey. In Greek. Someday, I'm going to read the whole thing. He gave me so much, without promising me anything.

Goodbye, my darling, Ingvar.

We will always know.

We will always remember.

Goodbye.

MOIRA *(writing)* Allan, I feel like I have broken a promise to you, even if we never promised each other anything but to be faithful correspondents. For weeks at a time, I wondered if you were dead. But I have gone on living, as I must go on living, without him, and now probably without you. If you can take me as I am…

(to herself) No. I won't make any promises. I will never make any promises again.

ALLAN *(writing)* May 1st, 1945

Dear Moira,

I am sorry that I have not written sooner. I finally received today your letter of March 8th. It had gone astray during the past few weeks, which have been very eventful ones for me. I must tell you that I am in no position to judge you about the Mr.…

(to himself) The Norwegian Romeo. Whatshisname…

MOIRA Norqvist.

ALLAN *(writing)* Norqvist. I know you have been mad at me, and I want you to brace yourself for the truth. You were right. I have had another involvement here in England. I'm sorry to be so blunt, and I'm not expecting you to be anything but mad, and I'm not expecting you to want to keep seeing me if I make it back. These two years have been hard enough without someone's affection, and letters simply wouldn't suffice. I fell in love with another woman, a Polish girl who had seen incredible suffering because she was Jewish.

MOIRA *(looks up, snaps)* As if I should care about *her* suffering!

ALLAN *(continues)* Her name was Grazina Mankowitz.

MOIRA *(to herself) Was?*

MOIRA continues reading ALLAN's letter.

She was a strange, sad young woman who was carrying a terrible burden. She was guilty of the crime of being alive, when almost everyone around her had been killed by the Nazis. She bore this without complaint until the news came out of Bergen-Belsen. When Grazina heard what the SS did to her own family, it was more than she could bear. She killed herself.

I write you these facts not so that you will forgive me, but so that you will understand something of what has been going on over here. If you still choose to continue corresponding, I will be very glad, and if not, I will understand.

I'm sorry this note is so blunt and to the point. I remain,

ALLAN *(writing)* Your affectionate friend,

Allan.

MOIRA folds up the letter, pauses, puts it in her bodice. Pause. She takes out the letter and begins reading it to herself again while ALLAN speaks.

(to audience) The last night she was alive, we were together in London. I think she was waiting until she could say goodbye. We went walking, and she took me into St. Paul's. I had never made it there, and it was sort of a joke between us. We went into the old cathedral, and we sat in one of the pews at the side. She kept staring at the images of Christ, the crucifixion. "I don't understand you Christians," she told me. "You worship this Jewish man who told you to abandon your money, to serve God, and to turn the other cheek when somebody strikes you. And you do this." And she handed me the telegram. From some friend of a friend who had been with her mother and her little sister at the end in Bergen-Belsen. Her whole family.

I became angry. At the Germans, at her family for dying, at her for shoving it in my face like that. I told her that it wasn't our fault, that we were the ones who were trying to stop the Nazis. We fought in the Cathedral, she told me the meanest things she could think of, about my family, my lovemaking, everything. We sat whispering in the church until the sexton came up and insisted we leave.

I walked her home, told her I'd stay with her, wanted to keep her company. She wouldn't let me. We said goodbye. I said, "I'll come tomorrow before my train up North." She sort of smiled and kissed me and let herself in. I slept at the "Y" that night. When I went round in the morning, the police were there. She had been found in her kitchen. The police said it was a lucky thing no one had come in with a lighted match. The funeral was yesterday. I had to miss it. We had an op.

Seventh Movement: War's End

MOIRA *(writing)* My Dear, Dear Allan,

At last I understand what Dr. Wilmot meant by a Bacchanal. I have been to one today.

ALLAN *(writing)* We got the news in the officers' mess and by the time we got outside, the erks were already streaming off the base into the cities. They'd just dumped their breakfast trays onto the floor and bolted.

MOIRA *(writing)* All of Edmonton, it seems, showed up downtown today to celebrate. I want to cherish that memory as long as I live. There was of course an official parade, and a ceremony over at the Legislature. But that wasn't the real celebration.

ALLAN *(writing)* I caught a truck into York. Men of all ranks screaming, laughing, hugging like maniacs… I lost my hat, but didn't care. Some Nervous Nellie who mentioned the Pacific theatre was lucky to escape with a bloody nose.

MOIRA *(writing)* The real celebration was along Jasper Avenue and on 101st street, where people simply went out of their minds with joy. The whole street was filled with people. They were hanging out of the shop windows, and out of the upper floor of the King Edward Hotel. They had climbed all the lampposts and they commandeered the streetcars, scores of young men sitting on top of the cars, I was afraid they'd be electrocuted.

ALLAN *(writing)* The civilians of York went crazy. For them it was the end of six years of anxiety, bombs, telegrams, rationing, and putting up with damn foreigners.

MOIRA *(writing)* People were drinking in the streets and shouting like maniacs. Someone would begin a song, and thousands of voices would join in. At one point, someone started a chorus of "The White Cliffs of Dover," and grown men around me were crying.

ALLAN *(writing)* If you didn't want to be kissed by strangers or filled with free beer, you may as well have gone home. It was one big blur of relief and happiness.

MOIRA *(writing)* But the best part of all, my darling, was the thought that you wouldn't be flying over Germany any more…

ALLAN *(writing)* I was in love with the world…

MOIRA *(writing)* …or at least not being shot at if you were.

ALLAN *(writing)* I thought of you.

Short pause.

MOIRA *(writing)* I have seen lots of pictures of the devastation of Germany by Allied planes. I feel terrible for the families who lived in those hulks of buildings, but most of all I just want you home and safe. But perhaps I'm getting ahead of myself. There is still talk that Canadians will now be transferred to the South Pacific to fight the Japanese. God how I hope that it will not be you. We have very much to talk about when you get home. Mostly I want you to know that I'm dying to see you, and that I hope you're feeling the same way.

Whatever has happened, we must try to be happy.

I can't wait to hear from you.

ALLAN *(reading MOIRA's letter)* Best Love, Moira.

(to audience) I'm luckier than most I guess,

Roy with his mangled face, and all the dead.

What will become of the Germans? Their whole country is turned into rubble. Of all us guys, experts in this terrible trade? They say there's going to be some jobs in commercial aviation, but I don't have much desire to fly.

I have seen my friends and colleagues explode, or get burned, or mangled. And you make this hole in your mind, where they all go. A little crater in your mind, and you build a fence around it, and that's where they are, the ones who never came back in the morning.

And what am I going to tell you about my life here, the rush of fear, the deliciousness of survival. About the fierce needs of the survivors.

I don't think I'll ever be able to hear a sermon or a lecture for the rest of my life without thinking: no this isn't the way it is, this isn't real life they're talking about, they don't understand anything that's half so sacred as the huge crater in my mind where all my friends went.

I just don't know how I'm going to find my way back home.

MOIRA *(to audience)* The war was tragic and terrible. So much death, so much loss. No way to measure the suffering. We are tortured by doubt about Peter. The Japanese apparently didn't treat their prisoners very well.

(to herself) The war was fun. We were part of the world for a while, and we learned a lot. "Eat your ice cream while it's on your plate," says the poet. And the war taught us to do that.

(as though in answer to an inquiry) What will I tell my daughters? That I was one of the lucky ones. That they should never give up what I gained. That they should love and be happy.

I'm building a home in my heart. Perhaps we'll be able to live there.

(writing) Dear Allan,

I don't understand what is happening. The Americans have dropped a single bomb on some place called Hiroshima and apparently destroyed the entire city.... It's a very chilling thought.

Everyone is sure Japan will now have to capitulate. At last, the suspense about Peter will be over.

I'm dying to see you.

ALLAN rushes to don his dress uniform.

ALLAN *(writing)* I'm coming home! With the Japs out of it, the conversion of our squadron has stopped. Thank God it's over.

MOIRA *(writing)* Oh, joy, Allan, he's alive, and he's coming home! We've heard that Peter is among the survivors. He was unable to communicate with us, but he's alive! I'm so delighted for Mother, and Dad looks ten years younger.

ALLAN *(writing)* The best news is that I won't be "shipping out." I've been chosen to fly one of our Lancs back.

(to himself) Jesus, get to the point…

(writing) Moira, I've been doing a lot of thinking…

MOIRA *(to herself)* I want to see him before I write another word.

ALLAN *(to himself)* I think I have to do this in the flesh.

Final Scene: Homecoming

MOIRA's parents' farm.

ALLAN crosses the stage, for the first time coming into MOIRA's acting area. She comes forward to him, as though finding him unexpectedly on her porch.

ALLAN The train was early. I walked from the station.

MOIRA Come in. Mother's not home. Do you want…?

They are both standing.

You must think I'm a hypocrite.

Pause.

I'm sorry. It was too hard for me alone.

ALLAN Me too. I mean, I'm sorry too.

MOIRA You survived. You look older. Bigger.

ALLAN You've grown up.

MOIRA We all have. *(beat)* Do you have plans?

ALLAN I'm going to go back to university. They're offering settlements. I'll study something bland, calm. Maybe accounting… dentistry. I want to have a nice house somewhere in a small town. I want a garden, and maybe a cottage on a lake somewhere. I want a family, four kids, two boys, two girls, who will be fat and smiling and spoiled.

MOIRA Yes…

ALLAN steps to her.

ALLAN I want you to take this ring, and to put it on your finger, and to say, Allan Staunton, I promise to be your wife, for ever and ever, till death do us part.

He offers her the ring. It is the ring he had in his pocket the last time they saw one another.

MOIRA Wait. I want you to say, I will not blame you, and I will try not to blame myself, for everything that these times have made us do to ourselves…

ALLAN I don't…

MOIRA …or I will not marry you.

ALLAN I will not…

MOIRA …blame you…

ALLAN …blame you…

MOIRA …and I will try not to blame myself…

ALLAN …and I will try not to blame myself…

MOIRA For everything these times have made us do to ourselves.

ALLAN I may have nightmares.

MOIRA That's all right.

ALLAN I mean, for a long time.

MOIRA That's. All. Right.

ALLAN puts the ring on her finger.

Allan Staunton, I promise to be your wife, forever and ever, till death do us part.

ALLAN Let's begin.

MOIRA Yes, let's begin.

Lights out.

The end.

Kenneth Brown is one of Western Canada's most prolific writers for the theatre. Of his eight one-man shows, four have had national broadcasts in Canada and one in Germany, *Sparks* (*Feuer und Flamme*) and *North of America* (*Nach Manitoba*) have been translated into German, while *Life After Hockey* has been translated into French and German. As an actor, he has toured to nearly every place in the country large enough to support a theatre, and has toured in four countries abroad. Ken was trained at the National Theatre School and holds an MA from the University of Alberta. His teaching work at Grant MacEwan College in Edmonton has gained him friends and colleagues across the country, and lately he has devoted much time to directing and developing the works of young playwright-actors like Sheldon Elter (*Metis Mutt*), the Ribbit collective (*Be A Man, Be a Man With Girls*), and the up-and-coming Janel Snider. He also directed *Boy Groove*, Chris Craddock's brilliant boy band play. His most recent one-man show, *Lewis Lapham Live*, was based on the editorial writings of the brilliant Harper's editor who is one of the Bush Administration's most eloquent critics. Ken lives and works in Edmonton.

STEPHEN SCRIVER is known for his best-selling collection of hockey poems, *All Star Poet!* (Coteau, 1981), and has published three other books of poetry: *Between the Lines* (Thistledown, 1977), *More All Star Poet!* (Coteau, 1989) and *Under the Wings* (Coteau, 1991). His poetry has also been anthologised in *Number One Northern* (Coteau, 1976), *Diversions* (Alberta Education, 1978), *Contexts* (Gage, 1983), *The Maple Laugh Forever* (Hurtig, 1982), *100% Cracked Wheat* (Coteau, 1983), *A Sudden Radiance* (Coteau, 1988), and *In the Clear* (Thistledown, 1998). Stephen, who served as Sports columnist for *The Sports Line* in Edmonton between 1995-96, has also had poetry included in *88 Years of Puck-Chasing in Saskatchewan* (Schafer, 1977) and Ken Dryden's *Home Game* (M&S, 1989). In addition, his work in documentary film has been widely seen on History Television, especially "Missing On Way Back," which won a City of Regina Heritage Award and a Houston Film Festival Bronze Medal. He also helped research "Mountain of Gold" (History Television, 1999) and "Disasters of Canada" (History Television, 2000-01) six-part series. *Letters in Wartime* was his first serious foray into drama. He lives in Edmonton, where he has recently retired after 32 years of teaching, and lives with his wife of 33 years, Barbara, a midwife. They have three children and five grandchildren.